The 7th Child

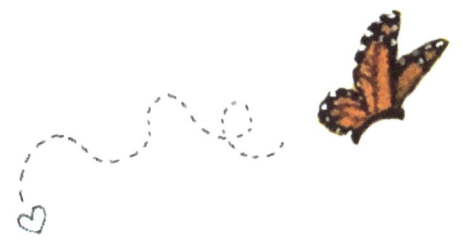

Story by Brenda Jenkyns
Artwork by Siren

Brenda Jenkyns: www.michaeljacksoneverafter.com
Siren: www.mjartbysiren.com

ISBN-13: 978-1519419217
ISBN-10: 151941921X

Special thanks to:
Carol Hodges
Wayne Van Tighem
Alexis Schlemm

For Michael, our Maestro

with L.O.V.E; BJ & Siren

A magical land once existed, closer to here than you might imagine. Breezes danced between the rivers, mountains, clouds and valleys, weaving a tapestry of beauty. Bright flowers and lush foliage painted the rolling hills in a masterpiece of color. The melodies of birds, the hum of dragonflies and bees, and the beat of water tumbling over rocks and waterfalls, joined in rhythm, the Music of Life. The whole land was alive with Magic.

The people of the land lived in harmony with all of nature and one another. A sacred connection existed between the people, and the One wholeness of Creation. Being held in those Beloved arms was their greatest Joy. The people expressed their deep love and gratitude for all they received, by giving their best in return. Listening to the call of their hearts and allowing the playfulness of life to flow through them, they shared their gifts. Some people chose to be artists, painters, sculptors, writers, poets, dancers, or musicians. Others were scientists, inventors, thinkers, or philosophers. Still others were drawn to being caregivers, builders, gardeners, or teachers. They were devoted to their chosen paths, challenging themselves to expand their knowledge and understanding by exploring new ideas and possibilities. Their lives were an adventure of discovery. Any obstacles they faced were viewed as opportunities, allowing the people to expand their souls by choosing love and compassion in every moment. The more of themselves they gave, the more Joy filled their hearts.

All forms of life were recognized as valuable and unique parts of the Oneness. Animals and plants were treated with reverence and respect. Nurturing and caring for nature, as it cared for them, ensured that there was no lack of any kind in the land. All was One wholeness of Joy.

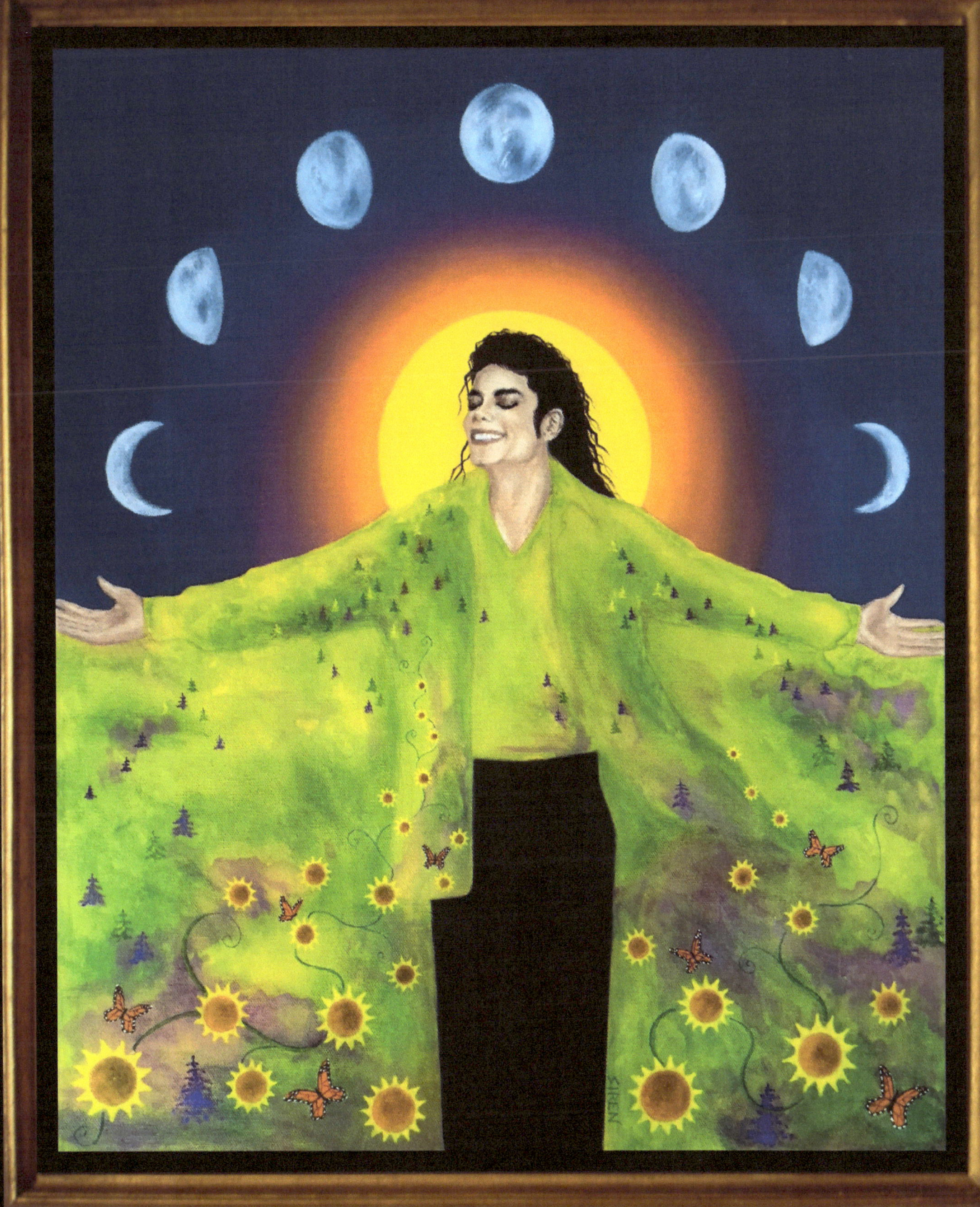

Spark Of Creation

In the midst of this pristine beauty, a woman rested in the shade of an ancient mango tree. She didn't hear the wind rustling in the leaves, or see the butterflies flitting among the flowers. Lost in her tangled thoughts, she was blind to the perfection and harmony around her. Although she lived in a land of extreme beauty and abundance, the woman did not feel the Joy within herself or her connection to the Oneness of life. Others seemed to know a secret that she was unaware of. She was not inspired to devote time or energy to finding her creative gift, or sharing herself with others. She felt left behind.

"What if...." A thought whispered in her mind. "What if this tree was MY tree?" The woman looked around quickly, wondering where the idea could have come from. She saw only the tree, butterflies, and a snake, peacefully resting in the shade of the branches.

"That's impossible," the woman thought, "nothing can be separated from the wholeness of everything."

"But what if it could be?" the whisper insisted. "What if......." The woman looked at the ripe mangos hanging in the tree. What if it WAS possible? What if she COULD step outside of the Oneness and be someone Special? If she owned this tree, she would no longer feel left behind. The more she thought about it, the more it seemed that the tree was already hers.

Just then, a child chasing butterflies, stopped to pick a mango from a low branch. The woman hesitated for a moment, then jumped up and shouted, "Stop! You can't have that, this is MY mango tree." The child was startled. How could this be? Was it possible for someone to OWN a tree? Dropping the fruit, the child ran to tell others what had happened. Soon, the story had spread across the land. Could it be true? What did it mean? Everyone who heard about this strange event stopped what they were doing, and for the first time, wondered what would happen next. Most people dismissed the impossible idea of owning nature, but some decided they should hurry and claim what they wanted for themselves, before others did.

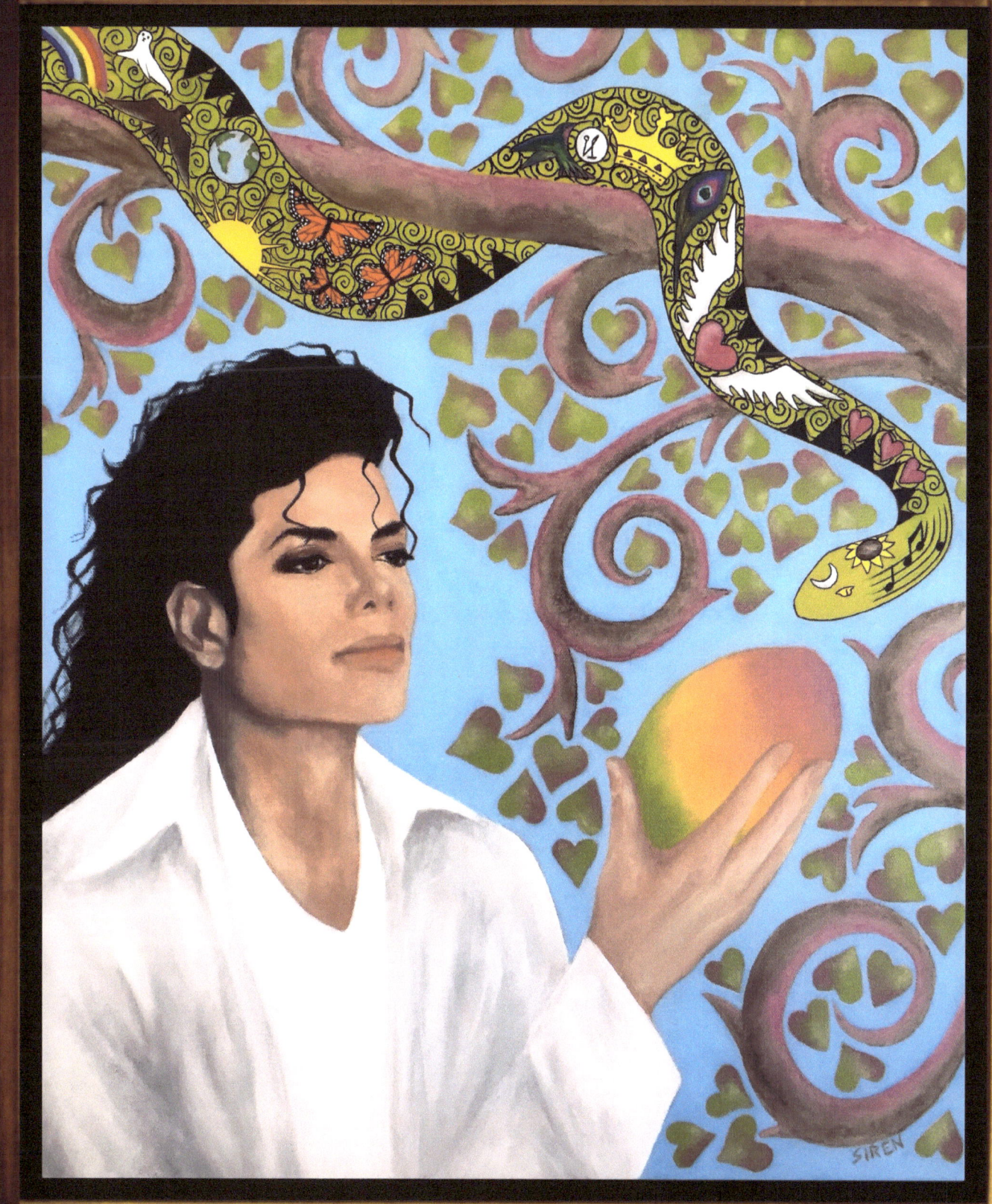

No Venom, No Hiss

This was the beginning of a different time in the land. The thought of separation gradually changed the minds and the hearts of the people. The belief in ownership of what had previously been shared by everyone, caused the people to become occupied with claiming what was theirs, keeping what they had, and trying to get more of what they wanted. The abundance that had been theirs for so long appeared to be gone. There now seemed to not be enough of anything.

The diversity that had enriched their lives now became cause for division. The people began to notice the differences between themselves and others, and separated into many groups according to these differences. The groups competed against each other and tried to take control of the water, the trees, the plants, the animals, and the land itself. This unnatural way of being was damaging to the perfect balance and harmony that nature had provided. The people no longer devoted themselves to what they loved most. They had forgotten how important their personal expression of Joy had once been to them. Their energy was now spent protecting themselves and their possessions. The people struggled. Everything suffered.

Some people took advantage of these changes and claimed a place of power and control. These people, who came to be called Medians, took it upon themselves to keep others in their groups. The people began to forget the Oneness that had been their foundation. Over many, many generations, the people of the land stopped appreciating how magical it was. They could no longer see the beauty all around them, although it was still there, as it had always been.

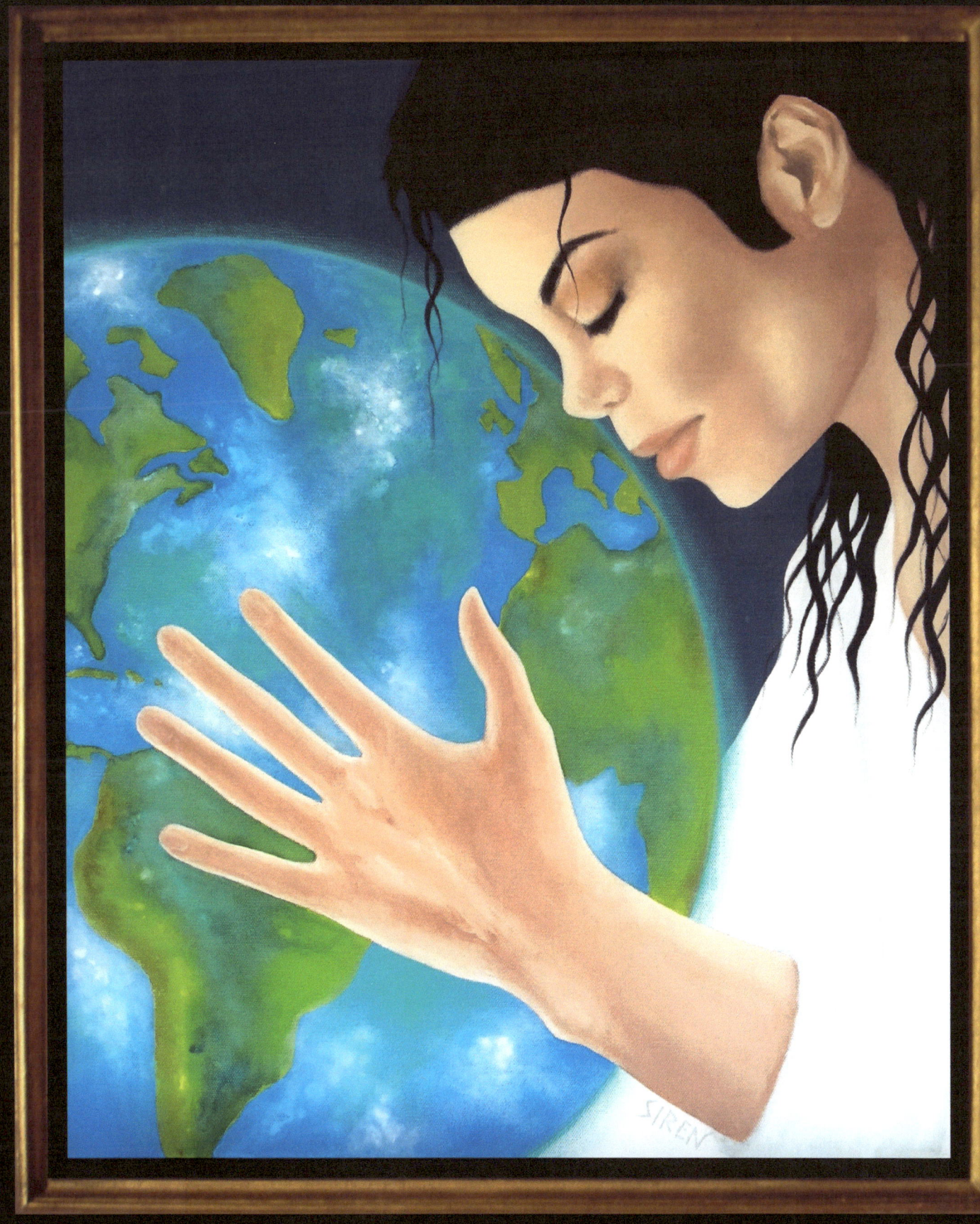

Exquisite Glow

The children of the land were born in the joy and innocence that came from belonging to the Oneness of Life. They were awake to the wonder around them and naturally trusted and loved others without fear. They lived in the moment, as children always had, easily believing in magic and open to all possibilities. They remembered their connection to nature and one another. As they learned the fractured way of life that had now become normal, the children gradually stopped believing in magic and saw the world as a competitive place. Their innocence faded away. Eventually, instead of sharing their hearts with one another, they separated themselves from the joys of childhood, and became like the adults around them.

Each child was encouraged to choose an occupation that would bring security and status to their family. Firstborn children had the most opportunity. They often became Medians, which was a prestigious position in society. Children in large families had fewer possibilities available to them, as there were limited resources to help them get ahead in life.

Around this time, a seventh child was born. Like all children, he loved to laugh and play, but there was something different about this child. He had a depth and serenity in his eyes that spoke of ancient wisdom. Beauty and joy was all he saw, and it reflected in everything he did. He absorbed the sights and sounds around him and wove them into beautiful music, lyrics, and dance. This was effortless and natural for him. The Source from which all Life flowed, was expressed through his pure heart and connection to Truth. He WAS the Oneness that had been forgotten. When he danced, he became the music. When he sang, he became the song.

The seventh child's expression of the soul was not recognized or appreciated. Art, in any form, was now considered unnecessary and useless in the land. What was the purpose of music and dance? It didn't bring food to the table or status to the family. It was hoped that the child would soon find a more useful way to spend his time.

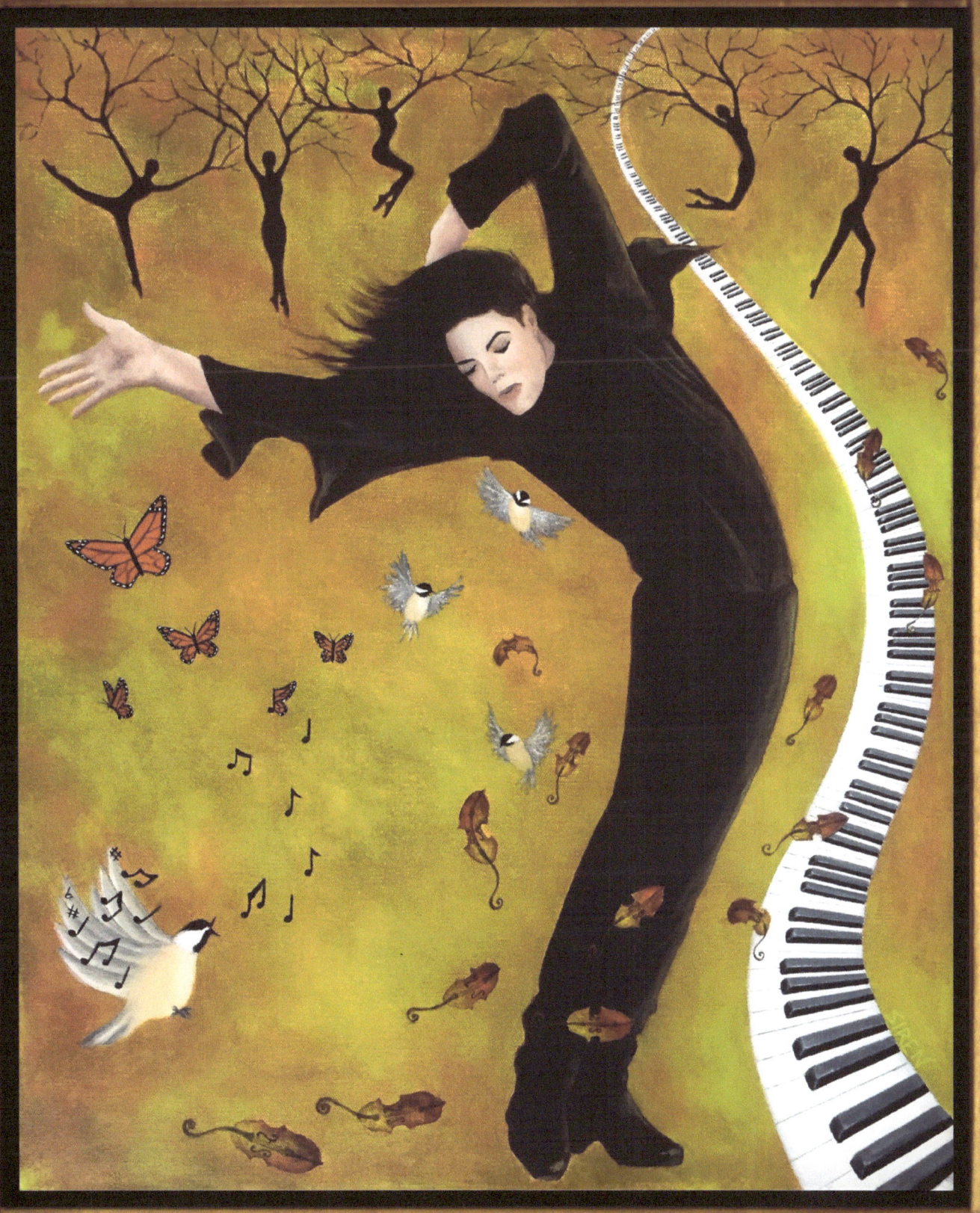

Music Of Life

The seventh child was not concerned about the expectations of others. He was listening to the Music of Life. His ideas and creativity were boundless. His Joy came from expressing his connection to his Soul, and sharing his gifts with others. His dream was to allow the magic and wonder that he saw to reveal the harmony and Love in all of Creation. If people could feel their connection to the Oneness of Life, the world could once again be a place of freedom and Joy. The seventh child demonstrated this Truth, through his life and his art. He danced, sang, and spoke of peace, love, Oneness, and caring for the land and one another.

His music brought joy to others and inspired them to believe in themselves. His energy and compassion touched people deeply. The beauty and love he saw in everyone, allowed them to see it within themselves. Adults were reminded of what it had been like to be children. Children saw that it was possible to make their dreams come true. People started to remember their similarities instead of their differences. Soon the seventh child was known as Maestro all across the land because of the harmony he brought wherever he went. When in his presence, people loved one another and forgot the things that seemed to separate them.

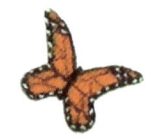

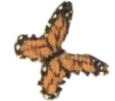

There were those who were not at all happy with what the Maestro was doing. The Medians' purpose in life was to ensure that everyone stayed in their groups and did what was expected. While the Maestro was a child, the Medians were not concerned about his unusual ways. They expected him to grow up and leave behind the magical world that he believed in. But as he matured, he continued to share his wonder and to inspire people to become more than they thought they could be. Instead of leaving childhood behind, he brought the power of innocence and trust into adulthood. Everything about him was a demonstration of kindness, understanding, and love for All.

As the Maestro continued to express his belief in Oneness and beauty, it became a problem to the Medians. He could no longer be confined to his own group. In fact, it wasn't even clear which group he belonged in anymore. He seemed to identify with ALL groups, and they with him. He did not allow himself to be limited or defined. He was the connection between everyone. He encouraged people to believe in themselves and have compassion for one another.

Although he was a seventh child, he became successful, and had many possessions and much respect and influence. This did not change the Maestro in any way. He remained humble and grateful for the recognition his life's work was receiving. He gave freely of everything he owned to those who had less. He saw no need to hold on to material possessions. This charitable way of being was completely unheard of in the land. The Maestro's followers increased in number and the people were beginning to awaken to their true nature of Love.

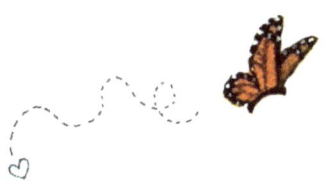

The Medians became concerned about their role as leaders of the people. With his unpredictable nature, no one could tell what the Maestro might do next. What he was demonstrating was the opposite of everything the Medians had worked to maintain. They felt threatened by this mysterious force that they could not control or understand. A meeting was held to discuss what should be done about the Maestro. They began to use their influence and power to discredit him. "Look at him," they told the people. "He doesn't look like us, he doesn't act like us, he doesn't think like us. He is not one of us. Who is this man? He is so different. He is an artist. He is a seventh child! He is not to be trusted."

The Maestro was aware of the Medians' actions, but he did not confront them or defend himself. He was connected to the deep wisdom of Life. He did not back down in exposing the harmful ways that had come to be acceptable. He chose to use the creative expression of his music to oppose the forces of hatred, fear, and mistrust that kept the people from recognizing their Oneness.

When the Medians saw that the Maestro was not going to conform, they worked even harder to stop him. They started rumors about him. They told stories that painted him as bizarre and weird. The people whose lives had been touched by the Maestro recognized these lies, but the land was big and there were those who listened to the Medians and started to believe what they said about the Maestro. Other people knew about the lies, but stayed quiet, not wanting to bring attention to themselves. Although he was loved all over the land, nothing was done to stop the Medians' efforts to harm the Maestro.

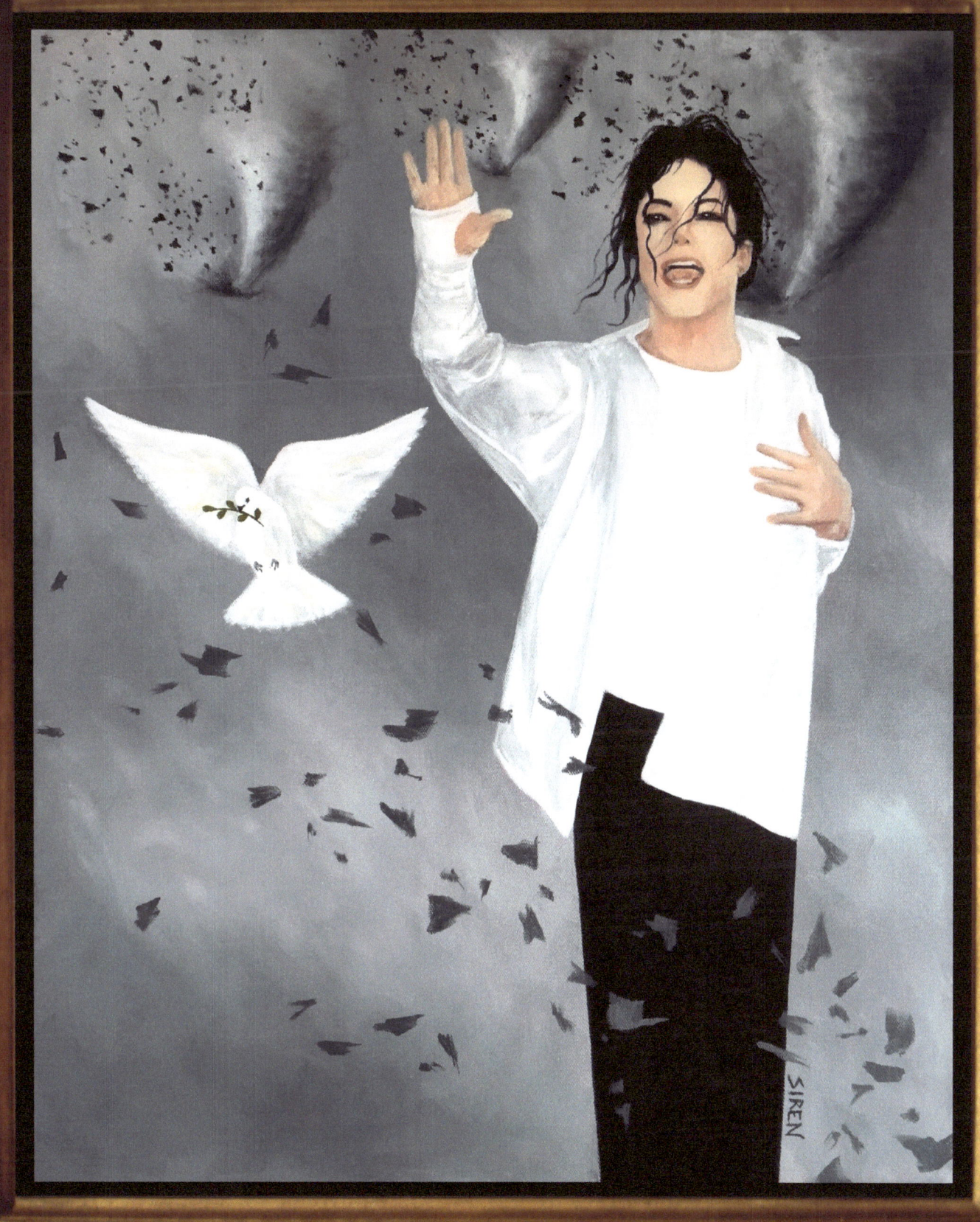

Power Of Innocence

The Maestro was not affected by the chaos around him. He WAS the Joy that he saw in everything. Sharing all he was continued to be his life. He especially loved being with children because they were most like him. Their simple goodness, honesty, and playfulness were his inspiration and hope. Some people thought he should protect himself from the Medians' attacks by conforming to their expectations, but standing up for Truth was what he had come to do, and he refused to compromise this in any way. He continued to be what he had always been, simple and sincere.

Next, the Medians tried to use the Maestro to make themselves rich and powerful. Some of them took advantage of his innocence and trust to get close to him, and took many of his possessions for themselves, but still he remained in a state of grace. Nothing that could be taken from him could change the truth of who he was.

The Medians held an emergency meeting. They were determined to find another way to turn the people against the Maestro. They conspired to influence a child to lie and say that the Maestro had hurt him. Even though the lie was exposed, this cruelty hurt the Maestro deeply. The very thing he loved most had been used against him. Even during this time of pain, the music within him flowed and he continued sharing his message of Love.

This angered the Medians. They decided to do everything they could to destroy him, once and for all. The Maestro did nothing to stop them. Love was the foundation of his music, his dance, and all that he was. He knew his power was of another Source. To willingly suffer the thorns of ignorance and fear, and continue to Love in return, was the way he demonstrated this Truth.

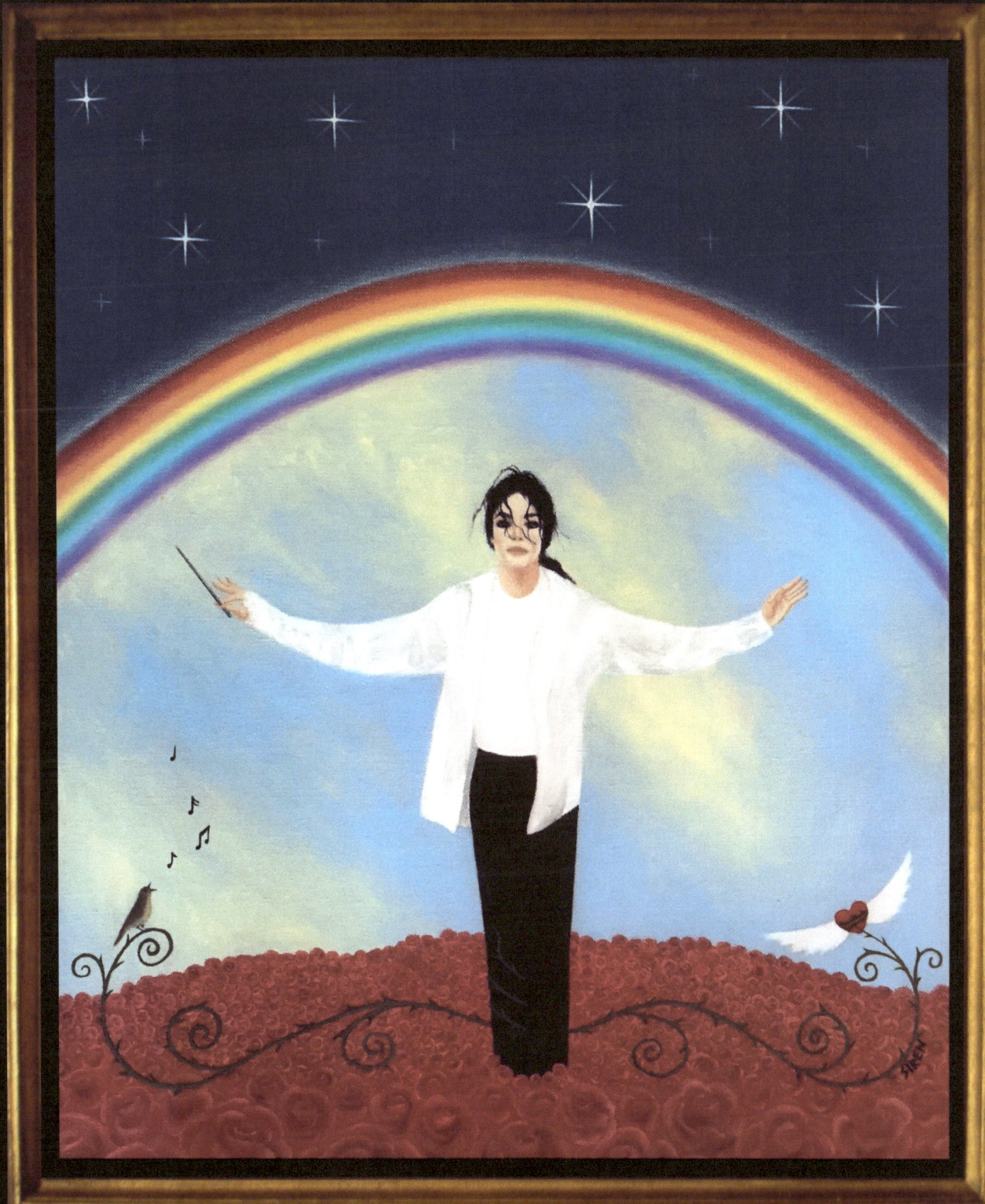

Mysterious Force

The Maestro devoted his life to giving all of himself to the world. Eventually, the time came when he chose to close his eyes for the last time and melt into the melody once again, in the form of pure Love. At that instant, an exquisite glow radiated out across the land, kindling Sparks of Creation within the hearts of people everywhere. The people looked at each other in a new way, and saw that there were no differences between them. The Knowledge of Oneness shone away thoughts of separation. They chose to devote their lives to becoming their true selves, inspired by the Maestro. They did this by expressing their creativity, and by loving one another as he had loved them. Many who hadn't known the Maestro in life felt their hearts open, and began to remember the Oneness that had been so long forgotten. The land was filled with artists, dancers, writers, bakers, teachers, healers, and endless other expressions of the Soul. The Dance of Life that the Maestro had demonstrated became their Truth. They were wrapped in His Beloved arms once again.

The abundance of the land began to return. The beauty in all things was again visible to those with eyes to see it. The Maestro had created a river of Living Water, weaving its magic across the land, returning it to peace and Joy. Although he appeared to be gone, the Maestro was closer than ever, inside each heart, waiting to be recognized.

The Maestro's dream continues. The people dance with Him, to the Music of Life, and give birth once again, to a magical land, closer to here than you might imagine.

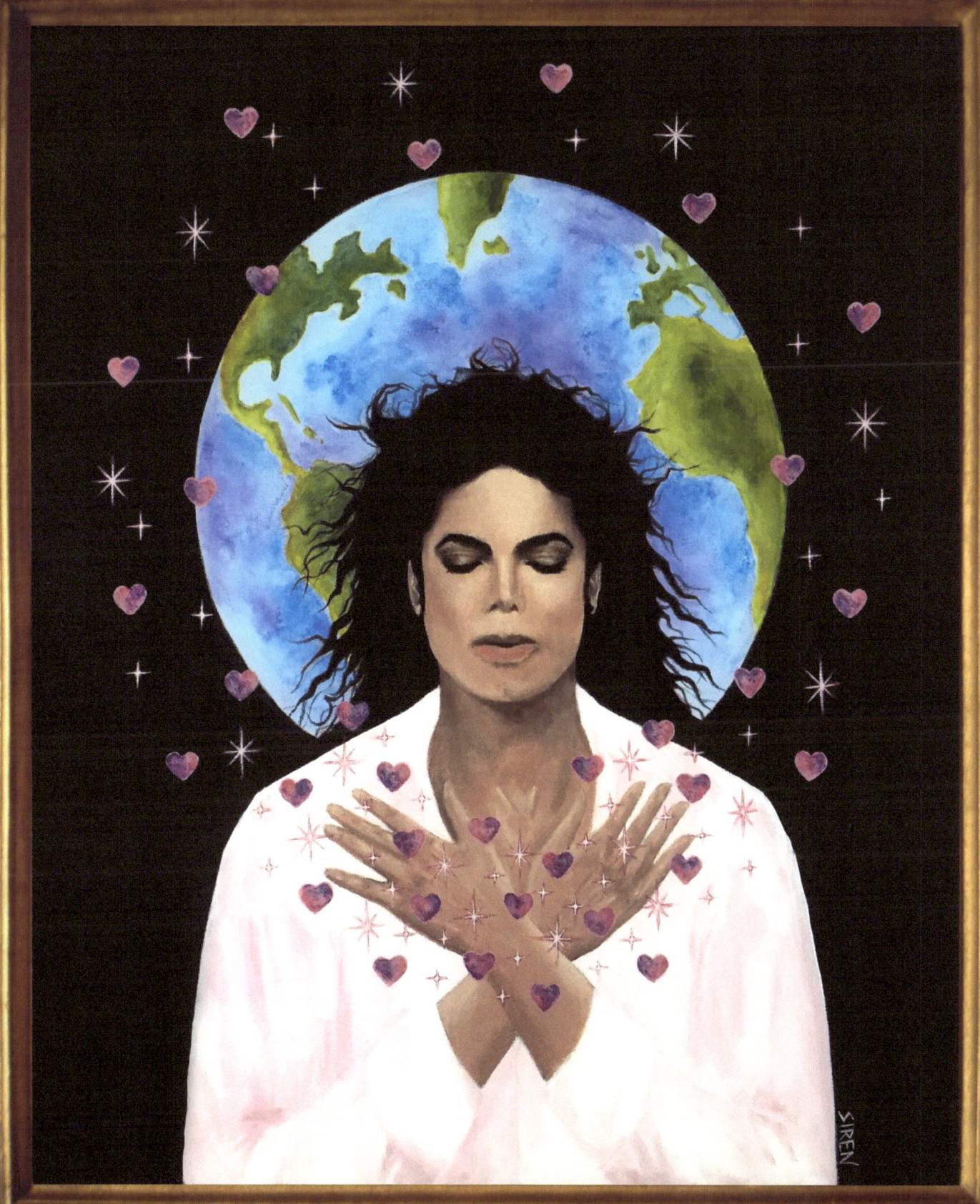

State Of Grace

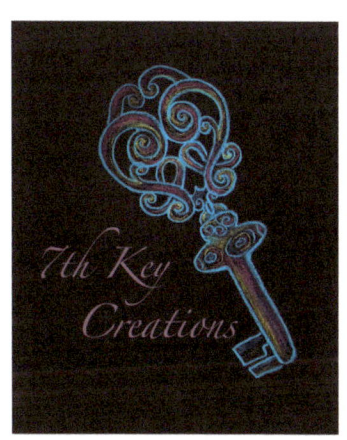

7thKeyCreations@gmail.com